MW01503816

CONTENTS

Understanding the MAP Tests

The NWEA MAP (Measures of Academic Progress) test is an adaptive assessment that is designed to measure student growth and progress in a variety of subject areas. The test is taken by millions of students across the United States and is widely used by educators to help inform instruction and measure student outcomes. The NWEA MAP test is administered online and provides immediate feedback on student performance, allowing teachers to adjust their teaching strategies and provide targeted support to individual students.

The NWEA MAP test is unique in that it is adaptive, which means that the difficulty of the questions adjusts based on the student's responses. This allows the test to be more personalized to each student's abilities and provides a more accurate measure of their knowledge and skills. The test covers a range of subject areas, including mathematics, reading, language usage, and science, and is administered multiple times throughout the school year. This allows teachers to track student progress and growth over time and make data-driven decisions to improve student outcomes.

Purpose and Benefits of MAP Testing

The primary purpose of the MAP Test is to provide valuable insights into a student's learning and academic progress. By offering a detailed analysis of a student's performance in reading, language usage, mathematics, and science, the test helps teachers tailor their instruction to meet individual needs. The MAP Test also serves as a benchmarking tool, allowing schools and districts to compare their students' performance with national norms and other local institutions.

This data-driven approach enables educators to make informed decisions about curriculum, instructional methods, and resource allocation, ultimately leading to improved student outcomes. Additionally, the MAP Test can help identify gifted students who may benefit from advanced or accelerated programs, as well as students who may require additional support or interventions.

Test Format and Content

The MAP Test is divided into four primary content areas: reading, language usage, mathematics, and science. Each section consists of multiple-choice questions that cover various topics and skills within the respective subject. The test is untimed, allowing students to work at their own pace and ensuring a lower level of test anxiety. The computer-adaptive nature of the MAP Test ensures that the difficulty of questions adjusts based on a student's performance, making it suitable for students of all ability levels. As a result, the MAP Test not only evaluates a student's mastery of grade-level content but also assesses their readiness for more advanced material.

Adaptive Testing and Scoring System

One of the unique aspects of the MAP Test is its adaptive testing system. As students answer questions, the test adjusts the difficulty of subsequent questions based on their performance. This adaptive nature allows the test to home in on a student's true ability level, providing more accurate and meaningful results. The MAP Test uses a RIT (Rasch Unit) scale to measure student achievement, which is an equal-interval scale that allows for easy comparison of scores across grade levels and subjects. This scoring system allows educators and parents to track a student's growth over time, making it an invaluable tool for understanding academic progress and setting individualized learning goals.

Preparing for Success on the MAP Test

Effective preparation for the MAP Test involves a combination of understanding the test format, mastering content knowledge, and developing test-taking strategies. This test prep book is designed to provide students with comprehensive guidance on each content area, offering targeted instruction and practice questions to build confidence and ensure success. Additionally, the book includes test-taking tips and strategies to help students approach the test with a calm and focused mindset. By working through this book and dedicating time to consistent practice, students will be well-equipped to excel on the MAP Test and achieve their academic goals.

Note that, since there is no cap to the level that a student can work to in preparation for this test, there is no 'completion' of content, as students can simply do questions from grades above in preparation. It should be noted that students are not expected to work far above grade level to succeed in this test, as consistent correct answers are more relevant.

What Is Contained Within this Book?

Within this book you will find 320 questions based off content which would be found within the MAP test your student will take. The content found in this book will be the equivalent of grade 1 level. Note that since this test is adaptive, some students may benefit by looking at several grade levels of content, not just their own.

At the end of the book will contain answers alongside explanations. It is recommended to look and check your answers thoroughly in regular intervals to make sure you improve as similar questions come up.

Topic 1 – Learning Base Words

1.1) What is the base word in 'happily'?

☐ happi

☐ hap

☐ happy

☐ happily

1.2) What is the base word in 'running'?

☐ runn

☐ run

☐ running

☐ runner

1.3) What is the base word in 'easier'?

☐ ease

☐ easy

☐ easi

☐ easier

1.4) What is the base word in 'baking'?

☐ baker

☐ baking

☐ bake

☐ bak

1.5) What is the base word in 'played'?

☐ play

☐ playing

☐ player

☐ played

1.6) What is the base word in 'painted'?

☐ painting

☐ paint

☐ painter

☐ paints

1.7) What is the base word in 'driving'?

☐ driver

☐ driving

☐ drived

☐ drive

1.8) What is the base word in 'walking'?

☐ walk

☐ walked

☐ walking

☐ walker

1.9) What is the base word in 'fishing'?

□ fishing

□ fisher

□ fish

□ fished

1.10) What is the base word in 'jumping'?

□ jumping

□ jumped

□ jumper

□ jump

1.11) What is the base word in 'cleaning'?

□ cleaning

□ cleans

□ cleaner

□ clean

1.12) What is the base word in 'laughing'?

□ laugher

□ laughing

□ laughs

□ laugh

1.13) What is the base word in 'thinking'?

□ thinks

□ think

□ thinker

□ thinking

1.14) What is the base word in 'crying'?

□ cries

□ cry

□ crying

□ cryer

1.15) What is the base word in 'dancing'?

□ dancer

□ dancing

□ dance

□ dances

1.16) What is the base word in 'smiling'?

□ smiler

□ smiling

□ smiles

□ smile

1.17) What is the base word in 'reading'?

□ read

□ reading

□ reads

□ reader

1.18) What is the base word in 'writing'?

□ write

□ writing

□ writer

□ writes

1.19) What is the base word in 'singing'?

□ sing

□ singer

□ sings

□ singing

1.20) What is the base word in 'building'?

□ building

□ builder

□ build

□ builds

1.21) What is the base word in 'watching'?

□ watch

□ watcher

□ watches

□ watching

1.22) What is the base word in 'playing'?

□ player

□ plays

□ playing

□ play

1.23) What is the base word in 'loving'?

□ loving

□ lover

□ loves

□ love

1.24) What is the base word in 'hopping'?

□ hopping

□ hops

□ hopper

□ hop

1.25) What is the base word in 'running'?

□ runs

□ runner

□ run

□ running

1.26) What is the base word in 'finding'?

□ finder

□ finding

□ finds

□ find

1.27) What is the base word in 'asking'?

□ asking

□ ask

□ asker

□ asks

1.28) What is the base word in 'talking'?

□ talks

□ talker

□ talk

□ talking

1.29) What is the base word in 'feeling'?

□ feeler

□ feeling

□ feels

□ feel

1.30) What is the base word in 'changing'?

□ changes

□ changing

□ changer

□ change

1.31) What is the base word in 'checking'?

□ checking

□ check

□ checks

□ checker

1.32) What is the base word in 'mixing'?

□ mix

□ mixer

□ mixes

□ mixing

1.33) What is the base word in 'fixing'?

☐ fixes

☐ fix

☐ fixer

☐ fixing

1.34) What is the base word in 'cooking'?

☐ cook

☐ cooker

☐ cooking

☐ cooks

1.35) What is the base word in 'washing'?

☐ wash

☐ washer

☐ washes

☐ washing

1.36) What is the base word in 'dreaming'?

☐ dream

☐ dreamer

☐ dreams

☐ dreaming

1.37) What is the base word in 'creating'?

□ creator

□ create

□ creating

□ creates

1.38) What is the base word in 'thinking'?

□ thinking

□ thinker

□ think

□ thinks

1.39) What is the base word in 'driving'?

□ drive

□ drives

□ drove

□ driver

1.40) What is the base word in 'crying'?

□ cryer

□ cries

□ crying

□ cry

Topic 1 – Answers

Question Number	Answer	Explanation
1.1	happy	"Happily" is derived from the base word "happy."
1.2	run	"Running" is derived from the base word "run."
1.3	easy	"Easier" is derived from the base word "easy."
1.4	bake	"Baking" is derived from the base word "bake."
1.5	play	"Played" is derived from the base word "play."
1.6	paint	"Painter" is derived from the base word "paint."
1.7	drive	"Driving" is derived from the base word "drive."
1.8	walk	"Walking" is derived from the base word "walk."
1.9	fish	"Fishing" is derived from the base word "fish."
1.10	jump	"Jumping" is derived from the base word "jump."
1.11	clean	"Cleaning" is derived from the base word "clean."
1.12	laugh	"Laughing" is derived from the base word "laugh."
1.13	think	"Thinking" is derived from the base word "think."
1.14	cry	"Crying" is derived from the base word "cry."
1.15	dance	"Dancing" is derived from the base word "dance."
1.16	smile	"Smiling" is derived from the base word "smile."
1.17	read	"Reading" is derived from the base word "read."
1.18	write	"Writing" is derived from the base word "write."

1.19	sing	"Singing" is derived from the base word "sing."
1.20	build	"Building" is derived from the base word "build."
1.21	watch	"Watching" is derived from the base word "watch."
1.22	play	"Playing" is derived from the base word "play."
1.23	love	"Loving" is derived from the base word "love."
1.24	hop	"Hopping" is derived from the base word "hop."
1.25	run	"Running" is derived from the base word "run."
1.26	find	"Finding" is derived from the base word "find."
1.27	ask	"Asking" is derived from the base word "ask."
1.28	talk	"Talking" is derived from the base word "talk."
1.29	feel	"Feeling" is derived from the base word "feel."
1.30	change	"Changing" is derived from the base word "change."
1.31	check	"Checking" is derived from the base word "check."
1.32	mix	"Mixing" is derived from the base word "mix."
1.33	fix	"Fixing" is derived from the base word "fix."
1.34	cook	"Cooking" is derived from the base word "cook."
1.35	wash	"Washing" is derived from the base word "wash."
1.36	dream	"Dreaming" is derived from the base word "dream."
1.37	create	"Creating" is derived from the base word "create."
1.38	think	"Thinking" is derived from the base word "think."
1.39	drive	"Driving" is derived from the base word "drive."
1.40	cry	"Crying" is derived from the base word "cry."

Topic 2 - Word Definitions

2.1) What does 'calm' mean?

☐ Very loud

☐ Really fast

☐ Extremely bright

☐ Peaceful and quiet

2.2) What does 'curious' mean?

☐ Very tired

☐ Scared

☐ Not interested

☐ Eager to know or learn something

2.3) What does 'discover' mean?

☐ Find something not known before

☐ Ignore something

☐ Lose something important

☐ Break something

2.4) What does 'enormous' mean?

☐ Very large or huge

☐ Moderately warm

☐ Extremely cold

☐ Very small

2.5) What does 'fair' mean?

☐ Unkind

☐ Equal and just for everyone

☐ Confusing

☐ Dishonest

2.6) What does 'ignore' mean?

☐ To run quickly

☐ To refuse to take notice of

☐ To shout loudly

☐ To pay close attention

2.7) What does 'jealous' mean?

☐ Feeling or showing envy of someone

☐ Liking to eat

☐ Wanting to sleep

☐ Feeling very happy

2.8) What does 'protect' mean?

□ To laugh at something

□ To keep safe from harm

□ To sing a song

□ To hurt someone

2.9) What does 'respect' mean?

□ To ignore advice

□ To play games

□ To dislike someone

□ Admiration felt or shown for someone

2.10) What does 'surprise' mean?

□ A boring task

□ A usual event

□ A known fact

□ An unexpected event

2.11) What does 'brave' mean?

□ Not scared

□ Very kind

□ Often silly

□ Feeling shy

2.12) What does 'fascinating' mean?

☐ Usually ignored

☐ Extremely interesting

☐ Somewhat dangerous

☐ Very boring

2.13) What does 'miserable' mean?

☐ Very unhappy

☐ Incredibly energetic

☐ Slightly annoyed

☐ Extremely happy

2.14) What does 'nervous' mean?

☐ Feeling excited

☐ Feeling worried or anxious

☐ Feeling relaxed and confident

☐ Feeling sleepy

2.15) What does 'ordinary' mean?

☐ Hard to find

☐ Unique and remarkable

☐ With no special features

☐ Invisible to the eye

2.16) What does 'proud' mean?

☐ Feeling pleased about something

☐ Feeling ashamed

☐ Feeling lost

☐ Feeling confused

2.17) What does 'question' mean?

☐ A command

☐ An answer

☐ An inquiry

☐ A statement

2.18) What does 'repeat' mean?

☐ To begin

☐ To leave

☐ To stop

☐ To do something again

2.19) What does 'searching' mean?

☐ Ignoring

☐ Destroying

☐ Building

□ Looking for something

2.20) What does 'spotless' mean?

□ Very dirty

□ Partially clean

□ Perfectly clean

□ Colorful

2.21) What does 'respect' mean?

□ Admiration

□ Indifference

□ Disrespect

□ Dislike

2.22) What does 'surprise' mean?

□ Something boring

□ Something planned

□ Something unexpected

□ Something usual

2.23) What does 'wonder' mean?

□ To ignore

□ To know everything

□ To feel curiosity

□ To dislike

2.24) What does 'shiny' mean?

☐ Really big

☐ Very bright

☐ Always slow

☐ Quite loud

2.25) What does 'joy' mean?

☐ A feeling of fear

☐ A feeling of anger

☐ A feeling of sadness

☐ A feeling of pleasure

2.26) What does 'protect' mean?

☐ To keep safe

☐ To expose

☐ To harm

☐ To ignore

2.27) What does 'precious' mean?

☐ Of great value

☐ Common

☐ Inexpensive

☐ Worthless

2.28) What does 'clean' mean?

□ Feeling tired

□ Never lost

□ Very old

□ Not dirty

2.29) What does 'miserable' mean?

□ Excited

□ Unhappy

□ Joyful

□ Comfortable

2.30) What does 'quick' mean?

□ Sleepy

□ Fast

□ Kind

□ Not at all

2.31) What does 'soft' mean?

□ Nice to touch

□ Loud and noisy

□ Feeling happy

□ Hard to hear

2.32) What does 'whisper' mean?

☐ To run quickly

☐ To yell loudly

☐ To jump high

☐ To speak softly

2.33) What does 'nervous' mean?

☐ Lazy and unmotivated

☐ Easily agitated

☐ Excited and energetic

☐ Calm and relaxed

2.34) What does 'proud' mean?

☐ Feeling lost

☐ Feeling confused

☐ Feeling ashamed

☐ Feeling happy about achievements

2.35) What does 'respect' mean?

☐ Jealousy of someone

☐ Dislike for someone

☐ Pity for someone

☐ Admiration for someone

2.36) What does 'silent' mean?

☐ Very busy

☐ Very happy

☐ No noise

☐ No time at all

2.37) What does 'unique' mean?

☐ Being the only one of its kind

☐ Being similar

☐ Being common

☐ Being ordinary

2.38) What does 'vibrant' mean?

☐ Sad and gloomy

☐ Dull and boring

☐ Full of energy

☐ Tired and sleepy

2.39) What does 'wise' mean?

☐ Experienced

☐ Foolish

☐ Careless

☐ Ignorant

2.40) What does 'zealous' mean?

☐ Apathetic

☐ Uninterested

☐ Lazy

☐ Enthusiastic

Topic 2 - Answers

Question Number	Answer	Explanation
2.1	Peaceful and quiet	"Calm" means not agitated or disturbed, peaceful.
2.2	Eager to know or learn something	"Curious" implies a desire to find out or learn something new.
2.3	Find something not known before	"Discover" means to find for the first time.
2.4	Very large or huge	"Enormous" means very big in size.
2.5	Equal and just for everyone	"Fair" implies being just and impartial.
2.6	To refuse to take notice of	"Ignore" means to deliberately not pay attention.
2.7	Feeling or showing envy of someone	"Jealous" means feeling envious towards someone else's success.
2.8	To keep safe from harm	"Protect" means to guard from danger or harm.
2.9	Admiration felt or shown for someone	"Respect" means to hold someone in high esteem.
2.10	An unexpected event	"Surprise" means something that happens unexpectedly.
2.11	Not scared	"Brave" means someone who is not scared of things.
2.12	Extremely interesting	"Fascinating" means very interesting.
2.13	Very unhappy	"Miserable" means feeling extremely unhappy.
2.14	Feeling worried or anxious	"Nervous" means experiencing worry or anxiety.
2.15	With no special or distinctive features	"Ordinary" means typical or usual, with no special features.
2.16	Feeling pleased about something	"Proud" means feeling satisfaction from one's achievements.
2.17	An inquiry	"Question" means to ask or inquire about something.
2.18	To do something again	"Repeat" means to do something again.
2.19	Looking for something	"Searching" means trying to find something.
2.20	Perfectly clean	"Spotless" means completely clean, without any spots.

2.21	Admiration for someone or something	"Respect" means holding someone or something in high regard.
2.22	Something unexpected	"Surprise" refers to something that is not anticipated.
2.23	To feel curiosity	"Wonder" means to be curious or amazed about something.
2.24	Very bright	"Shiny" means to be reflective and bright.
2.25	A feeling of pleasure	"Joy" means a state of great happiness.
2.26	To keep safe	"Protect" means to guard or defend from danger.
2.27	Of great value	"Precious" means of high value and worth.
2.28	Not dirty	"Clean" means something that is not dirty.
2.29	Very unhappy	"Miserable" means feeling a high degree of unhappiness.
2.30	Fast	"Quick" means something that moves very fast.
2.31	Nice to touch	"Soft" means something that is silky and nice to touch.
2.32	To speak softly	"Whisper" means to speak quietly and softly.
2.33	Easily agitated	"Nervous" means being easily worried or anxious.
2.34	Feeling happy about achievements	"Proud" means being satisfied with one's or others' achievements.
2.35	Admiration for someone	"Respect" means regarding someone highly for their qualities.
2.36	No noise	"Silent" means absolutely no noise at all.
2.37	Being the only one of its kind	"Unique" means being one of a kind or unlike anything else.
2.38	Full of energy	"Vibrant" means lively and full of vitality.
2.39	Experienced	"Wise" means being knowledgeable and prudent.
2.40	Enthusiastic	"Zealous" means being fervent or enthusiastic about something.

Topic 3 – Understanding Context Clues

Tommy found a strange gadget in his grandmother's attic. It was round, shiny, and had a big red button on it. He was very curious about what it could be. His grandmother told him it was a compass that helped adventurers find their way. Tommy imagined being an explorer, traveling to unknown places with the compass as his guide.

3.1) What does 'gadget' mean in the story?

□ A large machine

□ A piece of clothing

□ A small tool or device

□ A type of food

3.2) What does 'compass' mean in the story?

□ A device for finding direction

□ A type of book

□ A musical instrument

□ A tool for drawing circles

3.3) What does 'curious' mean in the story?

□ Angry about something

□ Bored with something

□ Wanting to know more about something

□ Scared of something

3.4) What does 'explorer' mean in the story?

□ A teacher

□ A person who never leaves home

□ Someone who travels to discover new places

□ A doctor

3.5) What does 'imagined' mean in the story?

□ To sing a song

□ To draw with a pencil

□ To create a picture in your mind

□ To forget something

In the garden, Mia saw a beautiful butterfly. It fluttered from flower to flower. Mia wondered why it moved that way. She asked her mom, who explained that the butterfly was pollinating the flowers. This means it was helping the flowers to grow seeds. Mia felt happy knowing the butterfly was helping nature.

3.6) What does 'fluttered' mean in the story?

□ To walk slowly

□ To wave or move lightly and quickly

□ To jump high

□ To sit down

3.7) What does 'pollinating' mean in the story?

☐ The process of transferring pollen to enable fertilization

☐ The process of planting new seeds

☐ The act of cutting the flowers

☐ The act of watering the plants

3.8) What does 'wondered' mean in the story?

☐ To forget

☐ To know everything

☐ To ignore

☐ To be curious or have questions about something

3.9) What does 'seeds' mean in the story?

☐ The fruit of a plant

☐ The small parts of a plant from which new plants grow

☐ The roots of a plant

☐ The leaves of a plant

3.10) What does 'helping' mean in the story?

☐ Giving assistance or support to someone or something

☐ Ignoring something

☐ Hurting something

☐ Destroying something

Lucy found a small, lost kitten under a park bench. The kitten was meowing softly, looking scared and hungry. Lucy decided to take the kitten home and care for it. She gave it some warm milk and a cozy blanket. The kitten soon felt safe and started purring happily. Lucy named her new friend 'Whiskers'.

3.11) What does 'lost' mean in the story?

☐ Sleeping deeply

☐ Playing happily

☐ Eating

☐ Unable to find the way

3.12) What does 'meowing' mean in the story?

☐ The way a dog barks

☐ Running fast

☐ The sound a cat makes

☐ Jumping high

3.13) What does 'scared' mean in the story?

☐ Feeling hungry

☐ Feeling excited

☐ Feeling bored

☐ Feeling frightened or afraid

3.14) What does 'cozy' mean in the story?

☐ Large and spacious

☐ Small and cramped

☐ Cold and uncomfortable

☐ Warm and comfortable

3.15) What does 'purring' mean in the story?

☐ Whistling

☐ Laughing

☐ The happy sound a cat makes

☐ Crying loudly

Every night, Ethan looked up at the stars, dreaming of flying among them. One evening, he saw a shooting star and made a wish. The next day, he found a mysterious map in his backyard leading to a hidden treasure. With excitement, Ethan followed the map, which took him on an adventure through the forest, across a river, and finally to a small cave where he discovered a chest filled with golden coins.Ethan realized that the real treasure was the journey and the memories he made.

3.16) What does 'shooting star' mean in the story?

☐ A star that dances

☐ A star that sings

☐ A star that is very bright

☐ A star that moves quickly across the sky

3.17) What does 'mysterious' mean in the story?

□ Difficult or impossible to understand

□ Loud and noisy

□ Soft and quiet

□ Very clear and easy to understand

3.18) What does 'treasure' mean in the story?

□ A toy

□ A chest of coins

□ A book

□ A single coin

3.19) What does 'adventure' mean in the story?

□ Sleeping

□ A regular school day

□ An exciting or very unusual experience

□ A boring day at home

3.20) What does 'journey' mean in the story?

□ Watching TV

□ Eating dinner

□ The act of traveling from one place to another

□ Staying in one place

Olivia had a garden filled with all sorts of flowers. One day, she noticed some of the flowers looked droopy and sad. She realized they needed more water. After watering them, the flowers perked up and bloomed beautifully. Olivia learned that taking care of plants requires attention and love. She felt proud as she watched her garden thrive.

3.21) What does 'droopy' mean in the story?

☐ Running quickly

☐ Hanging down; sagging

☐ Standing straight up

☐ Laughing loudly

3.22) What does 'perked up' mean in the story?

☐ Became tired

☐ Started crying

☐ Became cheerful or more lively

☐ Began to sleep

3.23) What does 'bloomed' mean in the story?

☐ To lose leaves

☐ To turn colors

☐ To fall down

☐ To produce flowers

3.24) What does 'thrive' mean in the story?

□ To stop growing

□ To disappear

□ To grow or develop well

□ To shrink

3.25) What does 'attention' mean in the story?

□ Notice taken of someone or something

□ Forgetting about something

□ Ignoring something

□ Disliking something

Max loved to play in the snow. One chilly winter day, he built a giant snowman in his backyard. He used carrots for the nose, coal for the eyes, and sticks for the arms. As the sun set, Max wrapped a scarf around the snowman's neck. He stepped back and admired his work, feeling a sense of accomplishment. Max's snowman was not just a figure made of snow; it was a symbol of winter joy and creativity.

3.26) What does 'chilly' mean in the story?

□ Extremely hot

□ Very windy

□ Quite sunny

□ Very cold

3.27) What does 'admired' mean in the story?

☐ Disliked intensely

☐ Regarded with respect or warm approval

☐ Ignored completely

☐ Destroyed quickly

3.28) What does 'accomplishment' mean in the story?

☐ A project that is postponed

☐ Something that has been achieved successfully

☐ An action without effort

☐ A task that has been failed

3.29) What does 'symbol' mean in the story?

☐ A story that is forgotten

☐ A literal object with no deeper meaning

☐ A song that is sung

☐ A thing that represents or stands for something else

3.30) What does 'creativity' mean in the story?

☐ Copying someone else's work

☐ Ignoring all rules and guidelines

☐ Following instructions without change

☐ The use of imagination or original ideas

Sarah and her friends decided to organize a picnic at the nearby park. They packed sandwiches, fruits, and lemonade. When they arrived, they found a perfect spot under a large oak tree. As they ate, they watched birds flying overhead and listened to the gentle rustle of leaves. The day was warm, and the soft breeze made it perfect for a day outside. They played games, laughed, and made wonderful memories together.

3.31) What does 'picnic' mean in the story?

☐ A meal eaten outdoors

☐ A meal cooked at home

☐ A formal dinner

☐ A fast food meal

3.32) What does 'rustle' mean in the story?

☐ A shout

☐ A musical note

☐ A soft, light sound of things gently rubbing together

☐ A loud noise

3.33) What does 'breeze' mean in the story?

☐ A storm

☐ A heatwave

☐ A strong wind

☐ A gentle wind

3.34) What does 'games' mean in the story?

☐ Chores

☐ Exercises

☐ Activities for amusement or competition

☐ Homework assignments

3.35) What does 'memories' mean in the story?

☐ Movies watched last week

☐ Plans for the future

☐ Books read recently

☐ Things remembered from the past

During a school field trip to the zoo, Kevin and his classmates visited various animal exhibits. Kevin was fascinated by the lions' roaring and the monkeys' playful antics. At the aquarium section, he was amazed by the colorful fish and the graceful jellyfish floating in the water. Kevin learned that each animal has unique habits and habitats. It was a day full of discovery and wonder, sparking Kevin's interest in wildlife conservation.

3.36) What does 'exhibits' mean in the story?

☐ Movies in a theater

☐ Books in a library

☐ Displays or presentations

☐ Plays on a stage

3.37) What does 'fascinated' mean in the story?

☐ Completely bored

☐ Greatly interested or attracted

☐ Slightly confused

☐ Somewhat interested

3.38) What does 'aquarium' mean in the story?

☐ A garden for flowers

☐ A place where water animals and plants are displayed

☐ A park for walking

☐ A library for books

3.39) What does 'habits' mean in the story?

☐ Rare events

☐ Unusual behaviors

☐ Regular practices or routines

☐ Occasional activities

3.40) What does 'conservation' mean in the story?

☐ The use of resources without care

☐ Ignoring environmental issues

☐ The protection and preservation of natural resources

☐ Focusing only on urban development

Topic 3 - Answers

Question Number	Answer	Explanation
3.1	A small tool or device	A gadget refers to a small mechanical or electronic device.
3.2	A device for finding direction	A compass is used to determine geographic direction.
3.3	Wanting to know more about something	Being curious means having a desire to learn or know more.
3.4	Someone who travels to discover new places	An explorer is a person who investigates unknown areas.
3.5	To create a picture in your mind	To imagine means to form a mental image or concept.
3.6	To wave or move lightly and quickly	Fluttered describes light, quick movement, like a butterfly's wings.
3.7	The process of transferring pollen to enable fertilization	Pollinating involves the transfer of pollen to allow plants to reproduce.
3.8	To be curious or have questions about something	Wondered means to think about something with curiosity.
3.9	The small parts of a plant from which new plants grow	Seeds are the reproductive part of a plant that can grow into a new plant.
3.10	Giving assistance or support to someone or something	Helping means providing aid or support.
3.11	Unable to find the way	Lost in this context means unable to find one's way.
3.12	The sound a cat makes	Meowing is the vocalization made by cats.
3.13	Feeling frightened or afraid	Scared means feeling fear or apprehension.
3.14	Warm and comfortable	Cozy means providing a feeling of warmth and comfort.
3.15	The happy sound a cat makes	Purring is a sound made by a content and happy cat.
3.16	A star that moves quickly across the sky	A shooting star is a meteor that burns up in the Earth's atmosphere, appearing as a streak of light.
3.17	Difficult or impossible to understand	Mysterious means something that is not easily understood or explained.
3.18	A chest of coins	The treasure was a chest of gold coins he found on his journey.

3.19	An exciting or very unusual experience	Adventure implies an undertaking with an uncertain outcome that is often exciting or daring.
3.20	The act of traveling from one place to another	Journey means the act of traveling from one place to another, often implying a long distance.
3.21	Hanging down; sagging	Droopy means bending or hanging down heavily.
3.22	Became cheerful or more lively	Perked up means to become more lively or cheerful.
3.23	To produce flowers	Bloomed means when a plant produces flowers.
3.24	To grow or develop well	Thrive means to grow vigorously or flourish.
3.25	Notice taken of someone or something	Attention means the act of focusing the mind on something.
3.26	Very cold	Chilly means noticeably cold.
3.27	Regarded with respect or warm approval	Admired means to regard with respect or warm approval.
3.28	Something that has been achieved successfully	Accomplishment refers to an achievement or success.
3.29	A thing that represents or stands for something else	Symbol means something used to represent something else.
3.30	The use of imagination or original ideas	Creativity refers to the ability to create or invent something original.
3.31	A meal eaten outdoors	Picnic refers to an outdoor meal where food is eaten in a scenic or informal setting.
3.32	A soft, light sound of things gently rubbing together	Rustle refers to the light sound made by things gently moving or rubbing together.
3.33	A gentle wind	Breeze means a light, gentle wind.
3.34	Activities for amusement or competition	Games refer to structured forms of play or competitive activities.
3.35	Things remembered from the past	Memories are recollections of past experiences or events.
3.36	Displays or presentations	Exhibits are displays or collections shown in a museum or zoo.
3.37	Greatly interested or attracted	Fascinated means being intensely interested or attracted.
3.38	A place where water animals and plants are displayed	Aquarium is a facility where aquatic animals and plants are kept and displayed.
3.39	Regular practices or routines	Habits refer to regular tendencies or practices, especially ones that are hard to give up.
3.40	The protection and preservation of natural resources	Conservation means the act of preserving, protecting, or restoring the natural environment and wildlife.

Topic 4 – Synonyms and Antonyms

4.1) What is a synonym for 'happy'?

☐ Fast

☐ Glad

☐ Tired

☐ Sad

4.2) What is the antonym of 'big'?

☐ Small

☐ Huge

☐ Giant

☐ Large

4.3) Which word means the same as 'fast'?

☐ Stop

☐ Drop

☐ Quick

☐ Slow

4.4) What is the opposite of 'full'?

☐ Packed

☐ Empty

☐ Filled

☐ Overflowing

4.5) Find a synonym for 'funny'.

☐ Boring

☐ Serious

☐ Hilarious

☐ Sad

4.6) What is a synonym for 'cold'?

☐ Chilly

☐ Hot

☐ Warm

☐ Dry

4.7) What is the antonym of 'soft'?

☐ Smooth

☐ Light

☐ Hard

☐ Gentle

4.8) Which word means the same as 'thin'?

☐ Thick

☐ Fat

☐ Heavy

☐ Slender

4.9) What is the opposite of 'new'?

☐ Recent

☐ Old

☐ Modern

☐ Fresh

4.10) Find a synonym for 'bright'.

☐ Shiny

☐ Dark

☐ Dull

☐ Dim

4.11) What is a synonym for 'light'?

☐ Bright

☐ Heavy

☐ Dull

☐ Dark

4.12) What is the antonym of 'high'?

☐ Short

☐ Above

☐ Tall

☐ Low

4.13) Which word means the same as 'strong'?

☐ Powerful

☐ Weak

☐ Light

☐ Fragile

4.14) What is the opposite of 'hard'?

☐ Sharp

☐ Soft

☐ Rough

☐ Heavy

4.15) Find a synonym for 'small'.

☐ Large

☐ Broad

☐ Tiny

☐ Huge

4.16) What is a synonym for 'wet'?

☐ Moist

☐ Arid

☐ Parched

☐ Dry

4.17) What is the antonym of 'early'?

☐ Soon

☐ Quick

☐ Rapid

☐ Late

4.18) Which word means the same as 'happy'?

☐ Upset

☐ Miserable

☐ Joyful

☐ Sad

4.19) What is the opposite of 'open'?

☐ Wide

☐ Closed

☐ Unlocked

☐ Ajar

4.20) Find a synonym for 'easy'.

☐ Simple

☐ Difficult

☐ Hard

☐ Complex

4.21) What is a synonym for 'large'?

☐ Narrow

☐ Tiny

☐ Huge

☐ Small

4.22) What is the antonym of 'rich'?

☐ Poor

☐ Wealthy

☐ Affluent

☐ Opulent

4.23) Which word means the same as 'quiet'?

☐ Loud

☐ Noisy

☐ Raucous

☐ Silent

4.24) What is the opposite of 'hard'?

☐ Rigid

☐ Stiff

☐ Tough

☐ Soft

4.25) Find a synonym for 'difficult'.

☐ Easy

☐ Simple

☐ Hard

☐ Straightforward

4.26) What is a synonym for 'angry'?

☐ Pleased

☐ Furious

☐ Joyful

☐ Happy

4.27) What is the antonym of 'up'?

☐ Down

☐ High

☐ Over

☐ Above

4.28) Which word means the same as 'short'?

☐ Lengthy

☐ Tall

☐ Long

☐ Brief

4.29) What is the opposite of 'begin'?

☐ Continue

☐ End

☐ Open

☐ Start

4.30) Find a synonym for 'stop'.

☐ Run

☐ Pause

☐ Go

☐ Move

4.31) What is a synonym for 'excited'?

☐ Bored

☐ Uninterested

☐ Tired

☐ Thrilled

4.32) What is the antonym of 'empty'?

☐ Full

☐ Hollow

☐ Vacant

☐ Clear

4.33) Which word means the same as 'wide'?

□ Thin

□ Slim

□ Broad

□ Narrow

4.34) What is the opposite of 'lose'?

□ Miss

□ Fail

□ Find

□ Win

4.35) Find a synonym for 'old'.

□ Ancient

□ Recent

□ New

□ Fresh

4.36) What is a synonym for 'scared'?

□ Calm

□ Brave

□ Frightened

□ Courageous

4.37) What is the antonym of 'above'?

☐ Below

☐ Top

☐ Over

☐ High

4.38) Which word means the same as 'clever'?

☐ Dumb

☐ Unwise

☐ Smart

☐ Silly

4.39) What is the opposite of 'give'?

☐ Offer

☐ Donate

☐ Take

☐ Provide

4.40) Find a synonym for 'quick'.

☐ Sluggish

☐ Slow

☐ Speedy

☐ Lazy

Topic 4 - Answers

Question Number	Answer	Explanation
4.1	Glad	"Glad" is a synonym for "happy," meaning feeling pleasure or contentment.
4.2	Small	"Small" is the antonym of "big," referring to something of lesser size.
4.3	Quick	"Quick" means the same as "fast," indicating rapid movement or speed.
4.4	Empty	"Empty" is the opposite of "full," meaning containing nothing.
4.5	Hilarious	"Hilarious" is a synonym for "funny," indicating something that causes laughter.
4.6	Chilly	"Chilly" is a synonym for "cold," referring to a slightly cold temperature.
4.7	Hard	"Hard" is the antonym of "soft," indicating something solid or firm.
4.8	Slender	"Slender" means the same as "thin," indicating something with small width or thickness.
4.9	Old	"Old" is the opposite of "new," referring to something that has existed for a long time.
4.10	Shiny	"Shiny" is a synonym for "bright," indicating something that reflects light or is luminous.
4.11	Bright	"Bright" is a synonym for "light," indicating something that emits or reflects light.
4.12	Low	"Low" is the antonym of "high," referring to something close to the ground or of lesser elevation.
4.13	Powerful	"Powerful" means the same as "strong," indicating something with great force or strength.
4.14	Soft	"Soft" is the opposite of "hard," indicating something that is easy to compress or lacks rigidity.
4.15	Tiny	"Tiny" is a synonym for "small," referring to something of very small size.
4.16	Moist	"Moist" is a synonym for "wet," indicating something slightly wet or damp.
4.17	Late	"Late" is the antonym of "early," indicating something happening after the expected or usual time.
4.18	Joyful	"Joyful" means the same as "happy," indicating a feeling of great pleasure or happiness.

ALEXANDER-GRACE EDUCATION

4.19	Closed	"Closed" is the opposite of "open," indicating something that is not open or is sealed.
4.20	Simple	"Simple" is a synonym for "easy," indicating something not complicated or difficult.
4.21	Huge	"Huge" is a synonym for "large," indicating something of great size or extent.
4.22	Poor	"Poor" is the antonym of "rich," referring to lacking in wealth or resources.
4.23	Silent	"Silent" means the same as "quiet," indicating the absence of sound.
4.24	Soft	"Soft" is the opposite of "hard," indicating something easily compressible or tender.
4.25	Hard	"Hard" is a synonym for "difficult," indicating something that requires a lot of effort or thought.
4.26	Furious	"Furious" is a synonym for "angry," indicating intense anger.
4.27	Down	"Down" is the antonym of "up," indicating a direction towards the ground.
4.28	Brief	"Brief" means the same as "short," indicating a short duration or length.
4.29	End	"End" is the opposite of "begin," indicating the conclusion or final part.
4.30	Pause	"Pause" is a synonym for "stop," indicating a temporary halt or cessation.
4.31	Thrilled	"Thrilled" is a synonym for "excited," indicating feeling excitement or pleasure.
4.32	Full	"Full" is the antonym of "empty," indicating something that contains as much as possible.
4.33	Broad	"Broad" means the same as "wide," indicating something with a wide extent from side to side.
4.34	Win	"Win" is the opposite of "lose," indicating achieving victory or success.
4.35	Ancient	"Ancient" is a synonym for "old," indicating something from a long time ago or of great age.
4.36	Frightened	"Frightened" is a synonym for "scared," indicating feeling fear or anxiety.
4.37	Below	"Below" is the antonym of "above," indicating a position lower than.
4.38	Smart	"Smart" means the same as "clever," indicating showing intelligence or good judgment.
4.39	Take	"Take" is the opposite of "give," indicating receiving or obtaining something.
4.40	Speedy	"Speedy" is a synonym for "quick," indicating fast movement or action.

Topic 5 - Reading Comprehension

One sunny day, Max and his dog, Buddy, went to the park. They played catch with a red ball. After playing, they sat under a big tree. Max shared his sandwich with Buddy. Then, they saw a duck in the pond. Max and Buddy had a wonderful day at the park.

5.1) What did Max and his dog play with?

□ A red ball

□ A green bike

□ A yellow frisbee

□ A blue kite

5.2) Where did Max and Buddy go?

□ To the zoo

□ To the school

□ To the store

□ To the park

5.3) What did Max share with Buddy?

□ A cookie

□ A sandwich

□ A piece of cake

□ An apple

5.4) What did they see in the pond?

☐ A fish

☐ A frog

☐ A duck

☐ A turtle

5.5) How was the day described?

☐ Wonderful

☐ Scary

☐ Tiring

☐ Boring

Lily found a tiny seed in her garden. She planted the seed in a small pot and watered it every day. Slowly, the seed grew into a beautiful flower. The flower was pink and smelled sweet. Lily was very proud of her flower and showed it to everyone.

5.6) What did Lily find in her garden?

☐ A big rock

☐ A colorful leaf

☐ A shiny coin

☐ A tiny seed

5.7) Where did Lily plant the seed?

☐ In the forest

☐ In a garden bed

☐ On the windowsill

☐ In a small pot

5.8) What color was the flower?

☐ Pink

☐ Yellow

☐ Blue

☐ Red

5.9) How did the flower smell?

☐ Sweet

☐ Spicy

☐ Sour

☐ Bitter

5.10) What did Lily do with her flower?

☐ She kept it secret

☐ She showed it to everyone

☐ She sold it

☐ She gave it away

Tommy went on a picnic with his family. They brought sandwiches, apples, and cookies. They laid a blanket under a large oak tree. Tommy saw squirrels playing and birds singing. After eating, they played tag and had a lot of fun. It was a great day for Tommy and his family.

5.11) Who went on a picnic?

☐ Tommy alone

☐ Tommy and his dog

☐ Tommy and his family

☐ Tommy and his friends

5.12) What did they bring to eat?

☐ Salad, chicken, and water

☐ Pizza, soda, and ice cream

☐ Burgers, fries, and milkshakes

☐ Sandwiches, apples, and cookies

5.13) Where did they lay the blanket?

☐ Under a large oak tree

☐ In the backyard

☐ By the river

☐ On the beach

5.14) What did Tommy see?

☐ Squirrels playing and birds singing

☐ Fish swimming

☐ Cats running

☐ Dogs barking

5.15) How was the day described?

☐ Great

☐ Terrible

☐ Okay

☐ Boring

Sara loves to draw. One day, she decided to draw her favorite park. She used green for the grass, blue for the sky, and yellow for the sun. She even drew her friends playing on the swings. When she was done, she showed her drawing to her family, and they loved it.

5.16) What does Sara love to do?

☐ Run

☐ Dance

☐ Draw

☐ Sing

5.17) What did Sara decide to draw?

☐ Her house

☐ Her favorite park

☐ Her pet

☐ Her school

5.18) What color did Sara use for the grass?

☐ Orange

☐ Purple

☐ Red

☐ Green

5.19) Who did Sara show her drawing to?

☐ Her teacher

☐ Her neighbors

☐ Her friends

☐ Her family

5.20) What was the reaction to Sara's drawing?

□ They were surprised

□ They disliked it

□ They loved it

□ They were indifferent

Every night, before bed, Mia reads a book. Last night, she read a story about a magical forest. In the forest, animals could talk, and trees could walk. Mia imagined herself playing hide and seek with the animals. The story ended with a grand feast for all the forest friends. Mia fell asleep dreaming about the magical forest. She loved the story so much that she read it over and over, which made her very happy.

5.21) What does Mia do every night before bed?

□ Watches TV

□ Listens to music

□ Plays video games

□ Reads a book

5.22) What was last night's story about?

□ A pirate adventure

□ A space journey

□ A hidden treasure

□ A magical forest

5.23) What special abilities did the animals and trees have?

□ They could disappear

□ They had super strength

□ They could fly

□ Animals could talk and trees could walk

5.24) What game did Mia imagine playing with the animals?

□ Soccer

□ Tag

□ Chess

□ Hide and seek

5.25) How did the story make Mia feel?

□ Excited

□ Happy

□ Bored

□ Scared

Danny loves exploring. One weekend, he decided to explore the hill behind his house. With a backpack full of snacks and a map, he set off on his adventure. Along the way, he found colorful flowers, interesting rocks, and even a hidden stream. At the top of the hill, Danny enjoyed the view of his town. He felt like a true explorer and couldn't wait for his next adventure.

5.26) What does Danny love doing?

□ Swimming

□ Painting

□ Exploring

□ Reading

5.27) Where did Danny decide to explore?

□ The beach

□ The city park

□ The hill behind his house

□ The forest

5.28) What did Danny take with him for the adventure?

☐ A backpack full of snacks and a map

☐ A camera and a notebook

☐ A kite and a frisbee

☐ A fishing rod and bait

5.29) What did Danny find on his way?

☐ A treasure chest

☐ An old castle

☐ Colorful flowers, interesting rocks, and a hidden stream

☐ A lost puppy

5.30) How did Danny feel at the top of the hill?

☐ Excited

☐ Tired

☐ Scared

☐ Happy

Emma and her grandmother bake cookies every Sunday. This Sunday, they decided to make chocolate chip cookies. They mixed the dough together, adding lots of chocolate chips. After baking, the kitchen smelled wonderful. Emma and her grandmother enjoyed the warm cookies with a glass of milk. It was a perfect end to their day.

5.31) Who bakes cookies together?

☐ Emma and her mother

☐ Emma and her friend

☐ Emma and her grandmother

☐ Emma and her brother

5.32) What type of cookies did they decide to make?

☐ Sugar cookies

☐ Peanut butter cookies

☐ Chocolate chip cookies

☐ Oatmeal raisin cookies

5.33) What did the kitchen smell like?

☐ Chocolate

☐ Wonderful

☐ Fresh flowers

☐ Citrus

5.34) What did Emma and her grandmother enjoy with the cookies?

☐ Tea

☐ Coffee

☐ Hot chocolate

☐ Milk

5.35) How did their day end?

☐ With a walk

☐ With a story

☐ With a movie

☐ Perfectly

Ben found a strange-looking rock in his backyard. It was shiny and had different colors. Curious, he took it to his science teacher the next day. The teacher explained that it was a quartz crystal. Ben was amazed to learn about crystals and minerals. He decided to start a rock collection.

5.36) What did Ben find in his backyard?

☐ A bird

☐ A flower

☐ A bug

☐ A rock

5.37) Who did Ben show the rock to?

☐ His mother

☐ His neighbor

☐ His science teacher

☐ His friend

5.38) What was the rock actually?

☐ A ruby

☐ A piece of glass

☐ A diamond

☐ A quartz crystal

5.39) What did Ben decide to start?

☐ A book club

☐ A sports team

☐ A rock collection

☐ A garden

5.40) How did Ben feel about learning of crystals and minerals?

□ Amazed

□ Confused

□ Scared

□ Bored

Topic 5 - Answers

Question Number	Answer	Explanation
5.1	A red ball	Max and Buddy played catch, specifically with a "red ball."
5.2	To the park	They went "to the park" for their activities.
5.3	A sandwich	Max shared "his sandwich" with Buddy.
5.4	A duck	They saw "a duck" in the pond at the park.
5.5	Wonderful	Their day at the park was described as "wonderful."
5.6	A tiny seed	Lily found "a tiny seed" in her garden, which she later planted.
5.7	In a small pot	She planted the seed "in a small pot."
5.8	Pink	The flower that grew from the seed was "pink."
5.9	Sweet	The flower smelled "sweet."
5.10	She showed it to everyone	Lily was proud of her flower and "showed it to everyone."
5.11	Tommy and his family	The picnic involved "Tommy and his family."
5.12	Sandwiches, apples, and cookies	They brought "sandwiches, apples, and cookies" to eat at the picnic.
5.13	Under a large oak tree	They laid the blanket "under a large oak tree" for the picnic.
5.14	Squirrels playing and birds singing	Tommy saw "squirrels playing and birds singing" during the picnic.
5.15	Great	The day was described as "great" for Tommy and his family.
5.16	Draw	Sara loves "to draw," which is her favorite activity.
5.17	Her favorite park	Sara decided to draw "her favorite park."
5.18	Green	For the grass in her drawing, Sara used the color "green."

5.19	Her family	Sara showed her drawing "to her family," who loved it.
5.20	They loved it	The reaction to Sara's drawing was that "they loved it."
5.21	Reads a book	Mia's nightly routine before bed includes "reading a book."
5.22	A magical forest	The story Mia read last night was about "a magical forest."
5.23	Animals could talk and trees could walk	In Mia's story, "animals could talk and trees could walk."
5.24	Hide and seek	Mia imagined playing "hide and seek" with the animals in the story.
5.25	Happy	Mia fell asleep dreaming about the magical forest, and read it over and over as it made her happy.
5.26	Exploring	Danny loves "exploring," which is his passion.
5.27	The hill behind his house	Danny decided to explore "the hill behind his house."
5.28	A backpack full of snacks and a map	For the adventure, Danny took "a backpack full of snacks and a map."
5.29	Colorful flowers, interesting rocks, and a hidden stream	On his way, Danny found "colorful flowers, interesting rocks, and a hidden stream."
5.30	Happy	At the top of the hill, Danny felt "happy," enjoying the view of his town.
5.31	Emma and her grandmother	"Emma and her grandmother" bake cookies together every Sunday.
5.32	Chocolate chip cookies	They decided to make "chocolate chip cookies" this Sunday.
5.33	Wonderful	After baking, the kitchen smelled "wonderful," filled with the aroma of cookies.
5.34	Milk	They enjoyed the warm cookies with "a glass of milk."
5.35	Perfectly	Their day ended "perfectly," implying satisfaction with their baking and time spent together.
5.36	A rock	Ben found "a rock" in his backyard, which he found interesting.
5.37	His science teacher	Ben showed the rock "to his science teacher" for more information.
5.38	A quartz crystal	The teacher explained that the rock was actually "a quartz crystal."
5.39	A rock collection	Inspired by what he learned, Ben decided to start "a rock collection."
5.40	Amazed	Ben felt "amazed" to learn about crystals and minerals, sparking a new interest.

Topic 6 – Introduction to Story Elements

In a colorful forest, there lived a happy rabbit named Ruby. Ruby loved exploring the forest, looking for new adventures. One day, Ruby found a hidden trail leading to a secret garden. In the garden, Ruby met a friendly bird named Bella. Together, they discovered a treasure chest filled with shiny stones. Ruby and Bella spent the day playing and exploring the garden, making a new friend in each other.

6.1) Who is the main character of the story?

☐ A friendly bird named Ruby

☐ A happy rabbit named Ruby

☐ A sad rabbit named Ruby

☐ A happy bird named Ruby

6.2) Where did the story take place?

☐ Near a treasure chest

☐ In a secret garden

☐ On a hidden trail

☐ In a colorful forest

6.3) What did Ruby find?

☐ A treasure chest filled with shiny stones

☐ A secret garden

☐ A happy rabbit

☐ A friendly bird

6.4) Who did Ruby meet in the garden?

☐ A mischievous fox

☐ A wise old tree

☐ A friendly bird named Bella

☐ Another rabbit

6.5) What did Ruby and Bella discover together?

☐ A treasure chest filled with shiny stones

☐ A map

☐ A magical flower

☐ A secret door

Max the mouse discovered a mysterious map in the attic of his house. The map led to a hidden treasure in the garden. Eager to find the treasure, Max set out on his journey. Along the way, he encountered various obstacles but also found helpful friends. Finally, Max found the treasure under the old oak tree. It was a box filled with delicious cheese. Max shared his treasure with his friends, celebrating their adventure.

6.6) Who found a mysterious map?

☐ A clever fox

☐ Max the mouse

☐ A brave lion

☐ A curious cat

6.7) Where did the map lead?

☐ To a hidden treasure in the garden

☐ To a secret cave

☐ To an island

☐ To the top of a mountain

6.8) What did Max find at the end of his journey?

☐ A box filled with delicious cheese

☐ A magical wand

☐ A box filled with gold

☐ A key to a secret door

6.9) Who did Max share his treasure with?

☐ His enemies

☐ No one

☐ His family

☐ His friends

6.10) How did the story end?

☐ With a celebration of their adventure

☐ With Max starting another journey

☐ With Max going to sleep

☐ With Max becoming a hero

Ellie the elephant loved to paint. One sunny day, she decided to paint the landscape outside her window. Using her trunk, she carefully mixed the colors and started painting the blue sky, green fields, and a bright yellow sun. When she finished, Ellie had created a beautiful masterpiece. She showed her artwork to her friends, and they were all amazed. Ellie felt proud and happy to share her joy of painting with others.

6.11) Who loved to paint?

□ A mischievous monkey

□ A thoughtful turtle

□ Ellie the elephant

□ A creative cat

6.12) What did Ellie decide to paint?

□ A portrait of her friend

□ A dream she had

□ The landscape outside her window

□ A bowl of fruit

6.13) How did Ellie paint?

□ With her tail

□ With her trunk

□ With her feet

□ With a brush in her mouth

6.14) What was the reaction to Ellie's painting?

☐ Her friends were amazed

☐ It made everyone laugh

☐ No one liked it

☐ It was ignored

6.15) How did Ellie feel after sharing her painting?

☐ Disappointed

☐ Angry

☐ Proud and happy

☐ Sad

Pablo the penguin lived at the South Pole. He was curious about the stars and wanted to learn more about them. One clear night, Pablo decided to stay up late to watch the stars. He saw constellations and even a shooting star. Excited, Pablo decided to make a scrapbook of all the stars he could see from his home. Soon, his friends joined him, and they all enjoyed stargazing together, sharing stories about the stars and the universe.

6.16) Who was curious about the stars?

☐ Lucy the leopard

☐ Gary the giraffe

☐ Sammy the seal

☐ Pablo the penguin

6.17) Where did Pablo live?

☐ In a dense forest

☐ In a big city

☐ At the North Pole

☐ At the South Pole

6.18) What did Pablo decide to do one clear night?

☐ Build a snowman

☐ Write a letter

☐ Go fishing

☐ Stay up late to watch the stars

6.19) What did Pablo create to remember the stars?

☐ A scrapbook

☐ A song

☐ A poem

☐ A painting

6.20) Who joined Pablo in his activity?

☐ His teacher

☐ His parents

☐ His friends

☐ Nobody

Cara the cat had a magical garden where flowers could sing and dance. Every morning, Cara would visit the garden to listen to the flowers' songs. One day, she discovered a new flower that could sing beautiful melodies. Fascinated, Cara decided to learn the song and sing along. Soon, the garden was filled with music, and all the animals came to listen. Cara and her magical flowers brought joy and harmony to everyone around.

6.21) Who had a magical garden?

□ Bella the bird

□ Cara the cat

□ Molly the mouse

□ Danny the dog

6.22) What was special about Cara's garden?

□ The flowers could sing and dance

□ It was always sunny

□ It was invisible

□ It had golden leaves

6.23) What did Cara discover one day?

□ A treasure chest

□ A new flower that could sing beautiful melodies

□ A talking tree

□ A hidden pond

6.24) What happened when Cara sang along with the new flower?

☐ The flower disappeared

☐ A rainbow appeared

☐ It rained

☐ The garden was filled with music

6.25) Who came to listen to the music?

☐ Nobody

☐ All the animals

☐ Only the birds

☐ Just Cara's friends

Oliver the owl loved reading books about adventures. One evening, he found an old book in the library that spoke of a hidden valley. Curious, Oliver decided to find this valley. Using clues from the book, he flew over mountains and rivers until he found the valley. It was more beautiful than he had imagined, with sparkling waterfalls and rare flowers. Oliver spent the night there, under the stars, dreaming of more adventures.

6.26) Who loved reading books about adventures?

☐ Sophie the squirrel

☐ Harry the hare

☐ Oliver the owl

☐ Mia the mouse

6.27) What did Oliver find in the library?

□ A treasure chest

□ A secret door

□ A magical map

□ An old book about a hidden valley

6.28) What did Oliver discover?

□ A hidden valley

□ A secret garden

□ An enchanted forest

□ A lost city

6.29) What was in the valley?

□ Sparkling waterfalls and rare flowers

□ A dragon

□ Ancient ruins

□ Gold and jewels

6.30) How did Oliver spend the night?

□ Under the stars

□ In a tree

□ In a cave

□ At an inn

Lucy the ladybug dreamed of flying to the moon. Every night, she would look up at the sky and wonder what it would be like. One day, she met a wise old beetle who told her about a special flower that could grant wishes. Lucy searched the meadow until she found the flower. She wished to fly to the moon, and suddenly, she found herself soaring through the stars. Lucy's adventure was magical, and she made many new friends in the sky before returning home with incredible stories to tell.

6.31) Who dreamed of flying to the moon?

☐ Lucy the ladybug

☐ Gerald the grasshopper

☐ Samantha the spider

☐ Peter the butterfly

6.32) Who told Lucy about the special flower?

☐ A friendly frog

☐ A curious cat

☐ A wise old beetle

☐ A singing bird

6.33) What could the special flower do?

☐ Sing beautiful songs

☐ Grant wishes

☐ Dance in the wind

☐ Change colors

6.34) Where did Lucy find herself after making the wish?

☐ Under the sea

☐ On top of a mountain

☐ Soaring through the stars

☐ In a deep forest

6.35) What did Lucy do before returning home?

☐ Collected shiny stones

☐ Learned to swim

☐ Made many new friends in the sky

☐ Found a treasure chest

Nina the squirrel had always wanted to sail across the lake. She built a small boat out of leaves and twigs. With a little sail made of a leaf, she set off on her journey. Along the way, Nina saw fish jumping and ducks swimming. As the sun set, she reached the other side of the lake. Nina felt proud of her achievement and looked forward to more adventures.

6.36) Who wanted to sail across the lake?

☐ Max the mouse

☐ Nina the squirrel

☐ Oliver the owl

☐ Lucy the ladybug

6.37) What did Nina use to build her boat?

□ Cardboard and tape

□ Leaves and twigs

□ Plastic bottles and rubber bands

□ Stones and mud

6.38) What did Nina see during her journey?

□ Turtles racing

□ Fish jumping and ducks swimming

□ Stars falling from the sky

□ Butterflies flying

6.39) What did Nina feel when she reached the other side?

□ Tired

□ Proud of her achievement

□ Lost

□ Scared

6.40) What does Nina look forward to?

□ More adventures

□ Going back home

□ Having a picnic

□ Building a house

Topic 6 - Answers

Question Number	Answer	Explanation
6.1	A happy rabbit named Ruby	Ruby is the main character who loves exploring the forest.
6.2	In a colorful forest	The story is set in a colorful forest where Ruby lives.
6.3	A secret garden	Ruby found a secret garden while exploring.
6.4	A friendly bird named Bella	In the garden, Ruby met Bella, a friendly bird.
6.5	A treasure chest filled with shiny stones	Together, they discovered a treasure chest with shiny stones.
6.6	Max the mouse	Max found the mysterious map in the attic.
6.7	To a hidden treasure in the garden	The map led Max to a hidden treasure in the garden.
6.8	A box filled with delicious cheese	Max found a box of delicious cheese as the treasure.
6.9	His friends	Max shared the treasure (cheese) with his friends.
6.10	With a celebration of their adventure	The story ended with a celebration among friends.
6.11	Ellie the elephant	Ellie loves to paint and is the main character.
6.12	The landscape outside her window	Ellie decided to paint the beautiful landscape she saw.
6.13	With her trunk	Ellie used her trunk to paint, showcasing her unique ability.
6.14	Her friends were amazed	Ellie's friends were amazed by her beautiful painting.
6.15	Proud and happy	Ellie felt proud and happy to share her artwork.
6.16	Pablo the penguin	Pablo was curious about the stars and the main character.
6.17	At the South Pole	Pablo lived at the South Pole and was fascinated by the stars.
6.18	Stay up late to watch the stars	Pablo decided to watch the stars, sparking his interest in them.

6.19	A scrapbook	Pablo created a scrapbook to remember the stars.
6.20	His friends	Pablo's friends joined him in stargazing and sharing stories.
6.21	Cara the cat	Cara had a magical garden where she met a singing flower.
6.22	The flowers could sing and dance	The garden was special because of the singing and dancing flowers.
6.23	A new flower that could sing beautiful melodies	Cara discovered a flower that sang beautifully.
6.24	The garden was filled with music	When Cara sang with the flower, the garden became musical.
6.25	All the animals	Animals came to listen to the music in the garden.
6.26	Oliver the owl	Oliver loved adventure books and discovered a hidden valley.
6.27	An old book about a hidden valley	Oliver found a book that led him to explore a hidden valley.
6.28	A hidden valley	Oliver's discovery was a beautiful and hidden valley.
6.29	Sparkling waterfalls and rare flowers	The valley had sparkling waterfalls and rare flowers.
6.30	Under the stars	Oliver spent the night dreaming of more adventures under the stars.
6.31	Lucy the ladybug	Lucy dreamed of flying to the moon and found a wish-granting flower.
6.32	A wise old beetle	A beetle told Lucy about the flower that could grant wishes.
6.33	Grant wishes	The special flower had the power to grant Lucy's wish.
6.34	Soaring through the stars	After making a wish, Lucy found herself flying among the stars.
6.35	Made many new friends in the sky	Lucy made friends in the sky during her magical adventure.
6.36	Nina the squirrel	Nina wanted to sail across the lake and is the main character.
6.37	Leaves and twigs	Nina used leaves and twigs to build her boat for the journey.
6.38	Fish jumping and ducks swimming	Nina observed fish and ducks during her journey across the lake.
6.39	Proud of her achievement	Nina felt proud after successfully sailing across the lake.
6.40	More adventures	Nina looks forward to having more adventures in the future.

Topic 7 – Spelling

7.1) Spell the word that means the opposite of 'cold'.

☐ hot

☐ hit

☐ hat

☐ hut

7.2) How do you spell the color of the sky and the ocean?

☐ blue

☐ blew

☐ bloo

☐ blu

7.3) What is the correct spelling for the number after nine?

☐ tin

☐ tun

☐ tan

☐ ten

7.4) Spell the word for a small, furry animal that says 'meow'.

☐ cat

☐ cot

☐ kat

☐ cut

7.5) How do you spell the name of the place where books are kept?

☐ lybrary

☐ liberry

☐ librery

☐ library

7.6) Which word is spelled correctly for something you wear on your head?

☐ hatt

☐ hat

☐ hut

☐ het

7.7) What is the correct spelling for the color of grass?

☐ grin

☐ grein

☐ grean

☐ green

7.8) Which word is spelled incorrectly?

☐ apple

☐ bananna

☐ orange

☐ grape

7.9) How do you spell the word for 'to jump over something'?

☐ leap

☐ liep

☐ leep

☐ leep

7.10) Which word is spelled correctly for a type of flower?

☐ rose

☐ rhose

☐ ruse

☐ roze

7.11) Which word is spelled correctly for something that shines in the night sky?

☐ starr

☐ star

☐ staar

☐ stur

7.12) What is the correct spelling for the act of running at a slow pace?

☐ joug

☐ jog

☐ jag

☐ jogg

7.13) Which word is spelled correctly?

□ happi

□ hapy

□ happpy

□ happy

7.14) How do you spell the word for 'a large body of water'?

□ laike

□ lake

□ laik

□ leik

7.15) Which word is spelled correctly for a type of bird?

□ crow

□ crouw

□ cro

□ croe

7.16) Which word is spelled correctly for a sweet fruit?

□ apple

□ aplle

□ aple

□ appel

7.17) How do you spell the word for 'a piece of furniture to sit on'?

□ chiar

□ chaire

□ chair

□ chare

7.18) Which word is spelled incorrectly?

□ book

□ penncil

□ desk

□ paper

7.19) What is the correct spelling for the sound a dog makes?

□ bork

□ bark

□ berk

□ burk

7.20) Which word is spelled correctly for a type of weather?

□ raine

□ rainy

□ rany

□ reiny

7.21) Which word is spelled correctly for a cold, sweet dessert?

☐ icecreem

☐ icecream

☐ ice cream

☐ ise cream

7.22) How do you spell the word for 'the opposite of light'?

☐ darck

☐ dork

☐ dark

☐ darc

7.23) Which word is spelled incorrectly?

☐ quit

☐ quite

☐ quiet

☐ quitt

7.24) What is the correct spelling for 'a body of water smaller than an ocean'?

☐ ce

☐ sei

☐ see

☐ sea

7.25) Which word is spelled correctly for something that bees make?

☐ hunny

☐ honey

☐ honney

☐ huney

7.26) Which word is spelled correctly for the part of the day after morning?

☐ afternoon

☐ afternon

☐ afternoone

☐ aftenoon

7.27) How do you spell the word for 'to move quickly on foot'?

☐ run

☐ runn

☐ rune

☐ ren

7.28) Which word is spelled correctly?

☐ friend

☐ fwend

☐ frend

☐ furend

7.29) What is the correct spelling for 'a place where animals live in the wild'?

☐ foreest

☐ forist

☐ forrest

☐ forest

7.30) Which word is spelled correctly for something you write with?

☐ penncil

☐ pencil

☐ pensil

☐ pencill

7.31) Which word is spelled correctly for something used to clean your teeth?

☐ tuthbrush

☐ toothbrash

☐ toothbrushe

☐ toothbrush

7.32) How do you spell the word for 'water that falls from the sky'?

☐ rayn

☐ rane

☐ rein

☐ rain

7.33) Which word is spelled incorrectly?

□ science

□ skool

□ scholar

□ school

7.34) What is the correct spelling for 'a small, round, green vegetable'?

□ pe

□ pae

□ pee

□ pea

7.35) Which word is spelled correctly for a type of fish?

□ sammon

□ salmon

□ salman

□ salmun

7.36) Which word is spelled correctly?

□ wallit

□ wolit

□ wallet

□ walet

7.37) Which word is spelled incorrectly?

□ headphones

□ scarf

□ dress

□ underwere

7.38) Which word is spelled incorrectly?

□ telephone

□ screen

□ radiator

□ pensil

7.39) What is the correct spelling for 'work you do after school'?

□ homewurk

□ homwork

□ homewirk

□ homework

7.40) Which word is spelled correctly

□ jackit

□ jahket

□ jacit

□ jacket

Topic 7 – Answers

Question Number	Answer	Explanation
7.1	hot	"Hot" is the opposite of "cold."
7.2	blue	"Blue" is the color of the sky and the ocean.
7.3	ten	"Ten" is the number after nine.
7.4	cat	"Cat" is a small, furry animal that says 'meow'.
7.5	library	"Library" is the place where books are kept.
7.6	hat	"Hat" is something you wear on your head.
7.7	green	"Green" is the color of grass.
7.8	bananna	"Bananna" is spelled incorrectly; the correct spelling is "banana".
7.9	leap	"Leap" means to jump over something.
7.10	rose	"Rose" is a type of flower.
7.11	star	"Star" shines in the night sky.
7.12	jog	"Jog" is the act of running at a slow pace.
7.13	happy	"Happy" is spelled correctly.
7.14	lake	"Lake" is a large body of water.
7.15	crow	"Crow" is a type of bird.
7.16	apple	"Apple" is spelled correctly for a sweet fruit.
7.17	chair	"Chair" is a piece of furniture to sit on.
7.18	penncil	"Penncil" is spelled incorrectly; "pencil" is correct.

7.19	bark	"Bark" is the sound a dog makes.
7.20	rainy	"Rainy" is spelled correctly for a type of weather.
7.21	ice cream	"Ice cream" is spelled correctly for a cold, sweet dessert.
7.22	dark	"Dark" is the opposite of light.
7.23	quitt	"Quitt" is spelled incorrectly; "quit" is correct.
7.24	sea	"Sea" is a body of water smaller than an ocean.
7.25	honey	"Honey" is something that bees make.
7.26	afternoon	"Afternoon" is the part of the day after morning.
7.27	run	"Run" means to move quickly on foot.
7.28	friend	"Friend" is spelled correctly.
7.29	forest	"Forest" is a place where animals live in the wild.
7.30	pencil	"Pencil" is something you write with.
7.31	toothbrush	"Toothbrush" is used to clean your teeth.
7.32	rain	"Rain" is liquid that falls from the sky.
7.33	skool	"Skool" is spelled incorrectly; "school" is correct.
7.34	pea	"Pea" is a small, round, green vegetable.
7.35	salmon	"Salmon" is a type of fish.
7.36	wallet	"Wallet" is spelled correctly.
7.37	underwere	"Underwere" is spelled incorrectly; "underwear" is correct.
7.38	pensil	"Pensil" is spelled incorrectly; "pencil" is correct.
7.39	homework	"Homework" is work you do after school.
7.40	jacket	"Jacket" is spelled correctly.

Topic 8 -Facts and Opinions

Tommy and his friends went to the park after school. They saw a big, colorful rainbow in the sky. Tommy said, 'That's the biggest rainbow I've ever seen!' His friend Lisa said, 'Rainbows happen when sunlight and rain meet.' Then, they saw some birds flying south. 'It means winter is coming,' Tommy stated. After playing for a while, Tommy declared, 'This is the best day ever!'

8.1) What did Tommy and his friends see in the sky?

☐ A big, colorful rainbow

☐ A flock of birds flying north

☐ Snow falling

☐ The sun setting

8.2) Why do rainbows happen, according to Lisa?

☐ Because of magic

☐ Whenever Tommy goes to the park

☐ When sunlight and rain meet

☐ When it snows

8.3) What did the birds flying south indicate?

☐ They are lost

☐ Summer is starting

☐ It's time for lunch

☐ Winter is coming

8.4) What did Tommy declare about the day?

□ He wants to go home

□ He saw a shooting star

□ He doesn't like rainbows

□ This is the best day ever!

8.5) Are Tommy's statements facts or opinions?

□ Opinions

□ Neither

□ Both

□ Facts

One sunny morning, Mia and her brother Alex decided to plant a garden. Mia said, 'I think flowers make the garden look beautiful.' Alex agreed and added, 'Sunflowers grow tall because they love the sun.' They planted roses, sunflowers, and daisies. While planting, Alex found a worm and said, 'Worms are scary.' Mia laughed and replied, 'Worms help the garden by keeping the soil healthy.' They worked all morning and felt proud of their garden.

8.6) What did Mia and Alex decide to do one sunny morning?

□ Paint a picture

□ Visit the zoo

□ Go for a bike ride

□ Plant a garden

8.7) What did Mia think makes the garden look beautiful?

☐ Garden gnomes

☐ Rainbows

☐ Butterflies

☐ Flowers

8.8) Why do sunflowers grow tall, according to Alex?

☐ They like the rain

☐ They love the sun

☐ They drink a lot of water

☐ They grow at night

8.9) What did Alex say about the worm?

☐ Worms are colorful

☐ Worms sing songs

☐ Worms can fly

☐ Worms are scary

8.10) How do worms help the garden, according to Mia?

☐ By scaring away birds

☐ By decorating the garden

☐ By keeping the soil healthy

☐ By watering the plants

During a weekend trip to the zoo, Ella and her cousin Noah saw many animals. Ella exclaimed, 'The lion's roar is the loudest sound in the world.' Noah pointed to the elephants and said, 'Elephants are the biggest animals that live on land.' They watched the monkeys swinging from trees and laughed at their funny faces. 'Monkeys are the funniest animals,' Ella said. Before leaving, they saw a peacock spreading its colorful feathers. 'Peacocks show their feathers to make friends,' Noah explained. They both agreed it was an amazing day at the zoo.

8.11) What did Ella and Noah visit during the weekend?

☐ The beach

☐ The zoo

☐ A museum

☐ A playground

8.12) What did Ella say about the lion's roar?

☐ It happens only at night

☐ It's the loudest sound in the world

☐ It can be heard miles away

☐ It scares all the animals

8.13) According to Noah, which are the biggest animals that live on land?

☐ Elephants

☐ Bears

☐ Rhinos

☐ Giraffes

8.14) What did Ella think about the monkeys?

☐ They can fly

☐ They like the cold

☐ They are the funniest animals

☐ They are very quiet

8.15) How did Noah explain peacocks spreading their colorful feathers?

☐ To sleep

☐ To swim

☐ To find food

☐ To make friends

Sarah and her grandmother baked cookies on a rainy day. 'Baking cookies is the most fun activity,' Sarah said with excitement. Her grandmother smiled and replied, 'Chocolate chip cookies are everyone's favorite.' They mixed the dough, added chocolate chips, and then watched the cookies bake in the oven. 'The smell of cookies is the best smell in the world,' Sarah declared. After the cookies were done, they enjoyed them with milk. 'This is the perfect way to spend a rainy day,' her grandmother agreed.

8.16) What did Sarah and her grandmother do on a rainy day?

☐ Painted pictures

☐ Read books

☐ Baked cookies

☐ Played board games

8.17) What did Sarah say about baking cookies?

☐ It takes too long

☐ It's very difficult

☐ It should only be done on sunny days

☐ It's the most fun activity

8.18) What did Sarah's grandmother say about chocolate chip cookies?

☐ They are everyone's favorite

☐ They are hard to make

☐ They don't taste good

☐ They are too sweet

8.19) What did Sarah declare about the smell of cookies?

☐ It's too strong

☐ It reminds her of the ocean

☐ It's the best smell in the world

☐ It's not pleasant

8.20) How did Sarah's grandmother describe spending a rainy day?

☐ The perfect way

☐ A waste of time

☐ Boring

☐ Too messy

Kevin and his dad went fishing early in the morning. 'Fishing is the best way to start the day,' Kevin's dad said as they set up their rods. Kevin was excited and hoped to catch a big fish. 'The early bird catches the worm,' he thought, remembering his dad's advice. After a while, Kevin caught a small fish and said, 'Every fish is a good catch.' His dad nodded, adding, 'Patience is the key to fishing.' They spent the whole morning by the lake and caught several fish. 'This was an unforgettable day,' Kevin concluded.

8.21) Where did Kevin and his dad go early in the morning?

□ Hiking in the mountains

□ Cycling in the park

□ Fishing by the lake

□ Swimming in the sea

8.22) What did Kevin's dad say about fishing?

□ It's the best way to start the day

□ It's too early for fishing

□ Fishing should be done at night

□ Fish are too hard to catch

8.23) What was Kevin's hope for fishing?

□ To swim with the fish

□ To see a whale

□ To catch a shark

□ To catch a big fish

8.24) What did Kevin say after catching a small fish?

☐ Every fish is a good catch

☐ Small fish aren't worth catching

☐ He wanted to go home

☐ Fishing is boring

8.25) How did Kevin conclude their fishing day?

☐ He prefers playing video games

☐ It was an unforgettable day

☐ He didn't enjoy it

☐ He thought it was too long

Lily and her family visited a farm during autumn. 'Pumpkins are the symbol of autumn,' Lily's mother remarked as they arrived. They saw many animals, but Lily was most excited to see the horses. 'Horses are the most graceful animals,' she said. Her brother disagreed, saying, 'No, swans are more graceful.' They picked apples and Lily thought, 'Apple picking is the best autumn activity.' Before leaving, they bought pumpkin pie. 'Pumpkin pie is the tastiest dessert,' Lily's father declared. They all agreed it was a wonderful day.

8.26) Where did Lily and her family go during autumn?

☐ The beach

☐ A farm

☐ A mountain

☐ A forest

8.27) What did Lily's mother say about pumpkins?

☐ They are the symbol of autumn

☐ They are too big

☐ They are the hardest to grow

☐ They don't taste good

8.28) What did Lily say about horses?

☐ They don't like people

☐ They can fly

☐ They are too noisy

☐ They are the most graceful animals

8.29) What did Lily think about apple picking?

☐ It's too hard

☐ It's boring

☐ Apples are not tasty

☐ It's the best autumn activity

8.30) What did Lily's father declare about pumpkin pie?

☐ It's too difficult to make

☐ It's not sweet enough

☐ It's the tastiest dessert

☐ He doesn't like it

On a bright Saturday morning, Jake and his sister Emma decided to make a lemonade stand. 'Lemonade stands are the best way to earn money,' Jake said confidently. Emma added, 'And lemonade is the most refreshing drink on a hot day.' They squeezed lemons, mixed water and sugar, and set up their stand. Their first customer said, 'This is the best lemonade I've ever tasted!' Emma believed, 'Friendly service is the key to a successful stand.' By the end of the day, they had sold all their lemonade. 'Today was a huge success,' Jake exclaimed.

8.31) What did Jake and Emma decide to do on a Saturday morning?

☐ Play video games

☐ Fly kites in the park

☐ Go to the beach

☐ Make a lemonade stand

8.32) What did Jake say about lemonade stands?

☐ They are the best way to earn money

☐ It's better to sell cookies

☐ People don't like lemonade

☐ They are too much work

8.33) What did Emma say about lemonade?

☐ It's too sour

☐ It's the most refreshing drink on a hot day

☐ It's not popular

☐ Water is better

8.34) What did their first customer say?

☐ This is the best lemonade I've ever tasted

☐ They need a bigger stand

☐ The lemonade is too sweet

☐ They should lower the price

8.35) What did Emma believe is key to a successful stand?

☐ A big sign

☐ Cheap prices

☐ Lots of flavors

☐ Friendly service

During science class, Mrs. Thompson showed her students different types of rocks. 'Rocks tell stories about the Earth,' she explained. Max was fascinated by the shiny quartz and declared, 'Quartz is the most beautiful rock.' His friend Zoe disagreed, saying, 'No, amethyst is more beautiful.' Mrs. Thompson then showed a piece of limestone and mentioned, 'Limestone is used in building materials.' After class, Max said, 'Science is the most interesting subject.' Zoe added, 'Especially when we learn about rocks!' They both looked forward to more science classes.

8.36) What did Mrs. Thompson show her students?

☐ Different types of rocks

☐ Types of animals

☐ Ways to recycle

☐ How to plant seeds

8.37) What did Max say about quartz?

☐ It's not valuable

☐ It's too common

☐ It can float on water

☐ It's the most beautiful rock

8.38) What did Mrs. Thompson say about limestone?

☐ It glows in the dark

☐ It's used in building materials

☐ It's the hardest rock

☐ It's the rarest rock

8.39) What did Max say about science class?

☐ It's too difficult

☐ It's the most interesting subject

☐ He prefers gym class

☐ It's boring

8.40) What did Zoe add about learning in science class?

☐ It's better with experiments

☐ She likes reading textbooks more

☐ Especially when we learn about rocks

☐ She prefers math class

Topic 8 – Answers

Question Number	Answer	Explanation
8.1	A big, colorful rainbow	They saw a rainbow in the sky, not birds flying north, snow falling, or the sun setting.
8.2	When sunlight and rain meet	Lisa explained the scientific reason for rainbows, not magic, Tommy's presence, or snow.
8.3	Winter is coming	The birds flying south indicate the approaching winter, not them being lost, the start of summer, or lunchtime.
8.4	This is the best day ever!	Tommy declared his enjoyment of the day, not a desire to go home, seeing a shooting star, or disliking rainbows.
8.5	Opinions	Tommy's statements are subjective opinions, not factual information.
8.6	Plant a garden	Mia and Alex decided to plant a garden, not engage in other activities.
8.7	Flowers	Mia thought flowers, not garden gnomes, rainbows, or butterflies, make the garden beautiful.
8.8	They love the sun	Alex believed sunflowers grow tall because of their love for the sun, not other reasons.
8.9	Worms are scary	Alex's reaction to the worm, not its color, singing, or ability to fly.
8.10	By keeping the soil healthy	Mia explained worms help the garden by keeping the soil healthy, not by other means.
8.11	The zoo	Ella and Noah visited the zoo, not the beach, museum, or playground.
8.12	It's the loudest sound in the world	Ella's exaggerated statement about the lion's roar, not its timing or effect on other animals.
8.13	Elephants	Noah pointed out elephants as the biggest land animals, not bears, rhinos, or giraffes.
8.14	They are the funniest animals	Ella found the monkeys' antics funny, not their ability to fly, like cold, or silence.
8.15	To make friends	Noah explained peacocks spread their feathers to make friends, not to sleep, swim, or find food.
8.16	Baked cookies	Sarah and her grandmother chose to bake cookies, not engage in other indoor activities.
8.17	It's the most fun activity	Sarah's opinion about baking cookies, not its difficulty or weather dependency.
8.18	They are everyone's favorite	Her grandmother's belief about chocolate chip cookies' popularity, not their difficulty or taste.

8.19	It's the best smell in the world	Sarah's opinion about the aroma of cookies, not its strength or unpleasantness.
8.20	The perfect way	Her grandmother's sentiment about spending a rainy day, indicating satisfaction.
8.21	Fishing by the lake	Kevin and his dad chose fishing as their morning activity, not hiking, cycling, or swimming.
8.22	It's the best way to start the day	Kevin's dad's positive view on fishing in the morning, not its timing or difficulty.
8.23	To catch a big fish	Kevin's hope during fishing, not other unrealistic goals.
8.24	Every fish is a good catch	Kevin's positive outlook after catching a small fish, not a focus on its size or boredom.
8.25	It was an unforgettable day	Kevin's summary of their fishing experience, indicating a positive and memorable day.
8.26	A farm	Lily and her family's autumn activity, not a visit to the beach, mountain, or forest.
8.27	They are the symbol of autumn	Lily's mother's comment about pumpkins, highlighting their seasonal significance.
8.28	They are the most graceful animals	Lily's admiration for horses, not her opinion on their dislikes, abilities, or noise level.
8.29	It's the best autumn activity	Lily's personal preference for apple picking during autumn, not a negative view.
8.30	It's the tastiest dessert	Lily's father's high praise for pumpkin pie, showing a preference for its flavor.
8.31	Make a lemonade stand	Jake and Emma's chosen activity, not playing video games, flying kites, or going to the beach.
8.32	They are the best way to earn money	Jake's confident assertion about lemonade stands as a means to earn money.
8.33	It's the most refreshing drink on a hot day	Emma's opinion on lemonade, highlighting its suitability for hot weather.
8.34	This is the best lemonade I've ever tasted	The first customer's positive feedback on the lemonade, indicating high quality.
8.35	Friendly service	Emma's belief in the importance of friendly service for the success of their stand.
8.36	Different types of rocks	The subject of Mrs. Thompson's lesson, focusing on geology, not animals, recycling, or planting.
8.37	It's the most beautiful rock	Max's personal opinion on quartz, emphasizing its aesthetic appeal.
8.38	It's used in building materials	Mrs. Thompson's factual statement about limestone's practical use, not its physical properties.
8.39	It's the most interesting subject	Max's enthusiastic view on science class, indicating his passion for the subject.
8.40	Especially when we learn about rocks	Zoe's specific interest in geology, showing a preference within the broader subject of science.

Ready for More?

The NWEA MAP testing is adaptive. This means that if your student found these questions too tricky or too easy, they may find it useful to practice grades below or above they grade they are in. This will expose students to new concepts and ideas, giving them a better chance at scoring higher in tests.

Alexander-Grace Education produces books covering Mathematics, Sciences, and English, to help your student maximize their potential in these areas.

For errata, please email
alexandergraceeducation@gmail.com

Made in the USA
Monee, IL
23 April 2025

16230655R00063